FACET BOOKS

SOCIAL ETHICS SERIES

230
T24w

56535

FACET fb BOOKS

SOCIAL ETHICS SERIES — 7

Franklin Sherman, General Editor

What Christians Stand For in the Secular World was originally
published in 1943 as a supplement to *The Christian Newsletter*.
The Problem of Power was first published in 1944
in *The Listener*. Both essays are here reprinted with
the kind permission of Mrs. William Temple.

Published by Fortress Press, 1965

INTRODUCTION © 1965 BY FORTRESS PRESS

Library of Congress Catalog Card Number 65-21081

2724D65   Printed in U.S.A.   UB3021

Introduction

WILLIAM TEMPLE, who died in October, 1944, only eighteen months after having been appointed Archbishop of Canterbury, will undoubtedly rank as one of the great figures of twentieth century church history. Author of several weighty tomes of philosophical theology, he was equally well-known as a prophet of social righteousness and a friend of the common people. Temple was born in 1881, son of an earlier Archbishop of Canterbury, Frederick Temple, and was educated at Oxford, where he later taught philosophy. Ordained a priest of the Church of England in 1914, he became Bishop of Manchester in 1921 and Archbishop of York in 1929. Throughout his life, William Temple was deeply involved in the ecumenical movement, and may be regarded as one of the chief architects of the World Council of Churches; at the time of his death he was serving as chairman of its Provisional Committee.

Books, lectures, and articles on Christian social ethics flowed continuously from Temple's pen, from his early

Introduction

Church and Nation, published in the midst of the First World War (London: Macmillan, 1915), to his radio talks and writings during the difficult days of World War II. These latter served as a kind of churchly counterpart to the speeches of Winston Churchill, nerving the British people for their struggle, while at the same time reminding them of the divine judgment on the "Christian civilization" they were defending, as well as on the means used to defend it.

Temple had his own very specific views about what social reforms were needed in his country, and never hesitated to express them, whether as priest, bishop, or archbishop. This may be seen, for example, in the final chapter and the appendix (entitled "A Suggested Program") of his *Christianity and Social Order,* which became a best-seller upon its publication as a paperback in 1942. His views were generally considered somewhat left of center, and in his earlier years he had been an avid supporter of the Labour Party. Temple always took pains, however, to distinguish between his own specific judgments about social policy or legislation, with which, as he recognized, other conscientious Christians might very well disagree, and those basic social *principles* which, he felt, all Christians must acknowledge. (Temple did not share the skepticism of many recent writers about the possibility of articulating such principles; i.e., his ethic was not purely "situational.") He spoke of principles such as "freedom," "fellowship," and "service," which sound rather vague, but which in Temple's hands become the tools of a relevant social criticism. The combination of freedom and fellowship,

Introduction

for example—i.e., respect for the person as person, combined with recognition of man's inherently social nature —rules out the extremes both of individualism and of collectivism in the political and economic order. The principle of service means that we should "use our wider loyalties to check the narrower"[1]; this implies a limit on the claims of corporations, labor unions, and similar subordinate groupings within the community.

The essay "What Christians Stand For in the Secular World" is to be understood against the background of this long-term interest of Temple's in working out a Christian consensus on social questions, a common Christian stance vis-á-vis the leading problems of the day. As J. H. Oldham emphasizes in his Preface, the importance of what is said in the essay lies not so much in the fact that Archbishop Temple says it, as in the fact that he believes these affirmations to represent an "observable convergence" among the views of thoughtful Christians in all denominations. Drafts of the document passed through various hands, and the finished product can be said to show the influence of Oldham himself, as well as of the thought of V. A. Demant (the latter particularly in section three of the essay).[2] But Temple

---

[1] *Christianity and Social Order* (3rd ed.; London: SCM Press, 1950), p. 70; cf. the whole chapter.

[2] J. H. Oldham, an English lay theologian, was a long-time friend and colleague of Temple both in social-ethical affairs and in the ecumenical movement. For examples of his thought, see Oldham, *Life in Commitment* (New York: Association [Reflection Books], 1959), and *Work in Modern Society* (Richmond, Va.: John Knox, 1961).

For the thought of V. A. Demant, see, for example, his essay "The Idea of a Natural Order," which first appeared in the volume edited by Maurice B. Reckitt, *Prospect for Christendom: Essays in Catholic Social Reconstruction* (London: Faber, 1945), and which is now scheduled for publication as a Facet Book.

Introduction

made all these thoughts very much his own. In the first paragraphs of the essay, he speaks autobiographically, hinting at the transition made in his own thought, over the years, from a more optimistic, philosophical form of Christianity (which he elsewhere called a "Christocentric metaphysic," and which stresses the incarnation) to a more realistic "theology of redemption" (which stresses the cross and resurrection).[3] This development brought Temple very close, in his later years, to the characteristic emphases of continental Protestant theology. Similarly, we may note that his insistence in the present essay and elsewhere on making a clear distinction between the tasks of citizen and churchman, and between the realms in which the norms of love and justice, respectively, are relevant, amounts to something very much like the Lutheran "two kingdoms" doctrine.

The essay "What Christians Stand For in the Secular World" first appeared as a supplement to the December 29, 1943, issue of *The Christian Newsletter,* a publication edited by J. H. Oldham on behalf of the group known as the Christian Frontier Council. The essay was reprinted in 1944 by the SCM Press, accompanied by Oldham's remarks as a preface.[4] The brief essay on "The Problem of Power" which is here appended ori-

---

[3] Cf. the "Chairman's Introduction" contributed by Temple to the volume *Doctrine in the Church of England: The Report of the Commission on Christian Doctrine Appointed by the Archbishops of Canterbury and York in 1922* (London: S.P.C.K., 1938), as well as his article "Theology Today," reprinted in *Thoughts in Wartime* (New York: Macmillan, 1940), pp. 93-107.

[4] Note the three questions put to the reader by Oldham in the Preface. It might be suggested that these questions, together with the five points of the essay itself, would form an excellent outline for group discussion of this material.

Introduction

ginated as a radio talk, one of the last that Temple gave, and was first printed in *The Listener* for November 2, 1944. It will be found to be a succinct and sympathetic treatment of a problem that still troubles many Christians, the question of the proper Christian attitude toward "power politics," both domestic and international. Combining this with what Temple has to say in the first essay about love and justice, we have the rudiments of an integrated view of the relations of love, power, and justice, a problem that has also recently occupied other Christian thinkers.[5]

[5] Cf. Paul Tillich, *Love, Power, and Justice: Ontological Analyses and Ethical Applications* (New York: Oxford University Press, 1954), and many of the works of Reinhold Niebuhr, whose profound influence on his own thought Temple freely acknowledged.

FRANKLIN SHERMAN

Mansfield College
Oxford, England
March, 1965

Contents

Preface *by J. H. Oldham*   1

1. What Christians Stand For in the Secular World   5

2. The Problem of Power   26

    For Further Reading   32

Preface

by J. H. OLDHAM

THE statement which follows originally appeared as a supplement to *The Christian Newsletter*. The Archbishop of Canterbury has written this statement in response to a request that he would take the initiative in trying to discover to what extent there exists a real and effective common Christian mind about the fundamental decisions which should govern the attitude and action of Christians in the secular world.

Its significance does not lie chiefly in the fact that the weight of its content and the authority of the writer give it unusual distinction. It is a different *kind* of document, and has a different purpose. What is of primary interest in this case is not simply that the Archbishop

What Christians Stand For in the Secular World

says these things, but that in saying them he believes, after testing the matter, that he is expressing an "observable convergence" among those who have given serious thought to the subject. Drafts of the paper were at various stages submitted to, and discussed with, persons representing widely different Christian traditions. These discussions seemed to show that the common ground is greater than is commonly recognized. The statement attempts to indicate what that common ground is.

If this basic agreement really exists about the fundamental choices to which Christians are committed, in sharp opposition to some of the dominant tendencies of our time, that fact may far outweigh in importance the differences which separate Christians about other matters. One of the greatest services that can be rendered to the Christian cause today may be to make this agreement stand out in bold relief so that it consciously controls and guides Christian thought and finds such vigorous expression in action that it becomes patent to all. If it were to permeate the consciousness of Christians, it would revivify all Christian activity by giving it a new common direction.

Readers will judge it differently according to the importance they attach to these three questions:

The first is whether there is in fact a body of common Christian conviction about what Christians stand for in the secular world. The statement maintains that such agreement already exists, at any rate in germ. But the consultation has not thus far been wide enough for a final conclusion; the paper is published to test the

What Christians Stand For in the Secular World

matter further. Further discussion will either disprove or confirm the fact of agreement.[1]

The second question is whether the proposed decisions are of such a nature as to compel those who make them to take sides in the actual, living conflicts of today. Unless they do that they are of no practical importance. The statement assumes, and in some points shows, that they do make that kind of difference. The decisions which the Archbishop puts forward are not theoretic propositions to which we can give an easy intellectual assent and then forget about them and pass on to some new interest. They have to do with the basic faith by which men live. They are what are sometimes called "existential" decisions, in which not only the mind, but our whole being, is involved. The answer has to be given not merely in thought, but in life.

The third question is, perhaps, the real crux. Are the proposed decisions significant and definite enough, sufficiently concrete and practical, to unite those who make them in a common loyalty, so that they become, in virtue of these commitments, a recognizable factor in public life and a force capable of influencing the course of history? Is it possible, that is to say, to find a real, living, and practically effective bond of union not in a common program but in a common *faith?*

The affirmations which the Archbishop proposes are all perceptions of the true nature of reality. They are

[1] Related essays were published intermittently in *The Christian Newsletter,* which unfortunately was never circulated widely in the United States, although files of it may be consulted in some theological libraries. In 1949 the *Newsletter* was merged into the quarterly journal *Frontier,* which is still being published and is available to American subscribers through the Eerdmans Publishing Co., Grand Rapids, Michigan.— EDITOR.

What Christians Stand For in the Secular World

religious affirmations rather than ethical, relating not to what ought to be, but to what *is*. Those who make them may easily disagree about practical programs, into which there inevitably enter judgments of facts about which opinions may diverge. The question, therefore, is whether the common religious beliefs are powerful and passionate enough to create a unity that transcends these differences.

1

WHAT CHRISTIANS STAND FOR IN THE SECULAR WORLD

THE distinction between the tasks of church and of society, of churchmen and citizens, is seldom clearly drawn; and the result is confusion and impotence. Either Christians try to act as churchmen in the world, only to find that the world refuses to be ordered on the principles proper to the church; or else they look out for the secular policy most congenial to their Christian outlook, only to find that their Christianity is a dispensable adjunct of no practical importance.

Church and state are different, though they may comprise the same people; and each has its own appropriate sphere and method. Churchman and citizen are words with a different connotation even when they denote the same person; and that person, the individual Christian, has to exercise both of these different functions. As long as he acts quite unreflectively he is likely to maintain the distinction and the appropriate balance fairly well, though he is also likely as a citizen to be excessively swayed by currents of purely secular thought and feeling. Moreover, it is almost impossible in these

What Christians Stand For in the Secular World

days to retain that naive spontaneity. Reflection or its fruits are thrust upon us, and when once that process has started it must be carried through. It is half-baked reflection which is most perilous.

In the nineteenth century men still assumed a law of God as universally supreme. In this country, at any rate, it was widely believed that God, whose nature was revealed in the Gospel and proclaimed by the church, was also the orderer of the world and of life; in only a few quarters was the alienation of the actual order from any subjection to the God and Father of Jesus Christ perceived or stated. The church was, therefore, free to concentrate its main energies on its distinctive task of proclaiming the Gospel of redemption, without any sense of incongruity with the ordering of life in the world outside. Theologians could undertake the task of showing that Christianity enables us to "make sense" of the world with the meaning "show that it *is* sense." And those of us who were trained under those influences went on talking like that; I was still talking like that when Hitler became Chancellor of the German Reich.

All that seems remote today. We must still claim that Christianity enables us to "make sense" of the world, not meaning that we can show that it is sense, but with the more literal and radical meaning of making into sense what, till it is transformed, is largely nonsense— a disordered chaos waiting to be reduced to order as the Spirit of God gives it shape. Our problem is to envisage the task of the church in a largely alien world. Some would have us go back to the example of the

What Christians Stand For in the Secular World

primitive church or of the contemporary church entering on an evangelistic enterprise in a heathen country; this means the abandonment of all effort to influence the ordering of life in the secular world and concentration of all effort upon what is, no doubt, the primary task of the church, the preaching of the Gospel and the maintenance among converts of a manner of life conformed to the Gospel. They advocate a spiritual return to the catacombs in the hope that the church may there build up its strength till, having kept the shield of faith intact and the sword of the Spirit sharp, it may come forth to a new conquest of a world which has meanwhile returned to a new dark age.

But this is a shirking of responsibility. The church must never of its own free will withdraw from the conflict. If it is driven to the catacombs it will accept its destiny and set itself there to maintain and to deepen its faith. But it cannot abandon its task of guiding society so far as society consents to be guided. It has a special illumination which it is called to bring to bear on the whole range of human relationships, and if, for lack of this, civilization founders, the church will have failed in its duty to men and to its Lord.

But if so, it must be active in two distinct ways. It must at all costs maintain its own spiritual life, the fellowship which this life creates, and the proclamation of the Gospel in all its fullness, wherein this life expresses itself. Here it must insist on all those truths from which its distinctive quality is derived—that God is Creator and man with the world his creature; that man has usurped the place of God in an endeavor to

What Christians Stand For in the Secular World

order his own life after his own will; that in the birth, life, death, resurrection, and ascension of Jesus Christ, God has himself taken action for the redemption of mankind; that in the Holy Spirit given by the Father through the Son to those who respond to the Gospel, power is offered for a life of obedience to God which is otherwise impossible for men; that those who are thus empowered by the Spirit are a fellowship of the Spirit or household of the Lord fitly called the church; that in that church are appointed means whereby men may receive and perpetually renew their union with their Lord and with one another in him, and so increase in the Holy Spirit. All this must be maintained and proclaimed. And unless the church is firm in its witness to its own faith, it will have no standing-ground from which to address the world.

But standing firm upon its own ground, it can and must address the world. By what convictions, constantly in mind, will Christians called to such a task direct their actions?

Basic Decisions

There is in fact more widespread agreement than is generally supposed with regard to these basic convictions. I do not mean that they are universally accepted among Christians; there are currents of Christian thought in all denominations which are directly opposed to some of them, and many devout Christians have as yet not turned their attention in this direction at all. But among Christians who have seriously and thoughtfully faced the historical situation with which we are dealing there is, as I have proved by testing, an observable convergence which may be presented in five affirmations. But as these are acts of faith, resting on a deliberate choice and involving a specific determination of the will, I speak of them rather as decisions.

1. *For God Who Has Spoken*

A vague theism is futile. The cutting edge of faith is due to its definiteness. The kind of deity established (if any is at all) by the various "proofs"—ontological, cosmological, and the like—is completely insufficient; it is usually little else than the rationality of the world presupposed in all argument about the world. The Christian has made a decision for God who has spoken —in nature, in history, in the prophets, in Christ.

It follows that the value of man and the meaning of history is to be found in the nature and character of God, who has thus made himself known. The value of a man is not what he is in and for himself (humanism), not what he is for society (fascism and communism), but what he is worth to God. This is the principle of Christian equality; the supreme importance of every man is that he is the brother for whom Christ died. This is compatible with many forms of social differentiation and subdivision. It is not compatible with any scheme which subjects a man's personality to another man or to any group of men such as the government or administrators of the state.

The purpose of God is the governing reality of history. Progress is approximation to conformity with it and fulfillment of it; deviation from it is retrogression.

What Christians Stand For in the Secular World

The nature of God is a righteousness which is perfect in love; his purpose, therefore, is the establishment of justice in all relationships of life—personal, social, economic, cultural, political, international. Many "humanists" share that aim, and Christians may well cooperate with them in practical policies from time to time. But a "decision for God" involves a sharp separation in thought, and, therefore, in the long run in practice, from many dominant tendencies of our time which seek the whole fulfillment of man's life in his earthly existence.

God has given to man freedom to decide for him or against him. This freedom is fundamental, for without it there could be only automatic obedience, not the obedience of freely offered loyalty. God always respects this freedom to the uttermost; therefore, freedom is fundamental to Christian civilization.

But though man is free to rebel against God, and can indeed do marvels through science and human wisdom in controlling his own destiny, yet he cannot escape the sovereignty of God. To deviate from the course of God's purpose is to incur disaster sooner or later—and sooner rather than later insofar as the deviation is great. The disaster ensues by "natural laws," as scientists use that phrase—that is, by the casual processes inherent in the natural order. But these laws are part of God's creation, and the disasters which they bring are his judgments.

Yet because man has so great a power to shape his own destiny he is responsible for using this. Belief in God is used by many Christians as a means of escape from the hard challenge of life; they seek to evade the responsibility of decision by throwing it upon God, who has himself laid it upon them. Faith in God should be not a substitute for scientific study, but a stimulus to it, for our intellectual faculties are God's gift to us. Consequently a decision for "God who has spoken" involves commitment to the heroic intellectual and practical task of giving to spiritual faith a living content over against the immensely effective this-worldliness of Marxism and secular humanism, while absorbing the elements of truth which these movements have often perceived more clearly and emphasized more strongly than Christians in recent times have done.

2. *For Neighbor*

As the first great commandment is that we love God with all our being, so the second is that we love our neighbor as ourselves. Here we are not concerned with that duty, but with the fact that underlies it whether we do our duty or not—not with what ought to be, but with what *is.* This is that we stand before God—that is, in ultimate reality—as bound to one another in a complete equality in his family. Personality is inherently social; only in social groupings can it mature, or indeed fully exist. The groupings must be small enough to enable each individual to feel (not only to think) that he can influence the quality and activity of the group, so that he is responsible for it, and also that it needs his contribution, so that he is responsible to it. He must feel that he belongs to it and that it belongs to him.

It is characteristic of much democratic thought that

What Christians Stand For in the Secular World

it seeks to eliminate or to depreciate all associations intermediate between the individual and the state. These, as the foci of local or other department loyalties, are nurseries of tradition and, therefore, obnoxious in the eyes of some prophets of progress. But it is in and through them that the individual exercises responsible choice or, in other words, is effectively free. The state is too large; the individual feels impotent and unimportant over against it. In his local, or functional, or cultural association he may count for something in the state, so that through his association he may influence the state itself, as alone he can scarcely do.

Thus the limitless individualism of revolutionary thought, which aims at setting the individual on his own feet so that he may, with his fellows, direct the state, defeats its own object and becomes the fount of totalitarianism. If we are to save freedom we must proceed, as Maritain urges,[1] from democracy of the individual to democracy of the person, and recollect that personality achieves itself in the lesser groupings within the state—in the family, the school, the guild, the trade union, the village, the city, the county. These are no enemies of the state, and that state will in fact be stable which deliberately fosters these lesser objects of loyalty as contributors to its own wealth of tradition and inheritance.

Christianity has always favored these lesser units.

---

[1] In many of his works; but see especially *Christianity and Democracy,* trans. Doris C. Anston (New York: Scribner, 1944), and *The Person and the Common Good,* trans. John J. Fitzgerald (New York: Scribner, 1947). Both of these volumes, although published subsequent to Temple's essay, were based on earlier writings by Maritain in French or English.—EDITOR.

What Christians Stand For in the Secular World

The Catholic church itself is composed of dioceses, in each of which the structure of the church is complete, representing the family of God gathered about the bishop as its father in God. And the civilization which the church most deeply influenced was characterized by an almost bewildering efflorescence of local and functional guilds of every sort.

The revolutionary and mechanistic type of thought finds its classical and fontal expression in Descartes' disastrous deliverance, *Cogito, ergo sum*.[2] Thus the individual self-consciousness became central. Each man looks out on a world which he sees essentially as related to himself. (This is the very quality of original sin, and it seems a pity to take it as the constitutive principle of our philosophy.) He sets himself to explore this world that he may understand and increasingly control it. In the world he finds a great variety of "things." He studies these in his sciences of physics, chemistry, and biology, according to their observable characteristics. Among the "things" are some which require a further complication of his method of study, giving rise to psychology. But though he is now allowing for instincts, emotions, sentiments, purposes, and similar factors, his attitude is the same as toward "things" which lacked these qualities. He organizes these psychological "things" in ways calculated to extract from them the result he desires. He may, for example, as an industrial manager, introduce welfare

[2] "I think, therefore I am." Cf. chapter III, "The Cartesian *Faux-Pas*," in Temple's Gifford Lectures, *Nature, Man and God* (New York: Macmillan, 1934).—EDITOR.

13

What Christians Stand For in the Secular World

work because he can in that way increase output. He might even, in an ultimate blasphemy, supply his troops with chaplains with no other object except to keep up military morale.

Now in all this he is treating persons as things. His relation to them is an "I-it" relation, not an "I-Thou" relation.[3] This latter he only reaches so far as he loves or hates, and only in this relation does he treat persons as they really are. He may do very much what the enlightened man of purely "scientific" outlook does: He provides for the welfare of employees, if he is an employer, and is, of course, glad that it pays. But that is not his motive; his motive is that they are human beings like himself. So he supplies what he would wish to have, and hopes and works for the time when they will not depend on him for what their welfare requires, but will be in a position to supply it to themselves. For he will prefer fellowship to domination.

It is in love and hate—the truly "personal" relationships—that we confront our neighbor as he is, a man like ourselves. Even hate has an insight denied to the egoist who coldly manipulates human beings as his pawns, and men resent it less. Most of us would rather be bullied than mechanically organized. But hate too is blind, partly from its own nature, partly because men hide from an enemy, as they do from a cynic, what is deepest and tenderest in their nature. Only love—the purpose of sheer good will intensified by sympathetic feeling—gives real insight and understanding.

---

[3] Cf. Martin Buber, *I and Thou*, trans. Ronald Gregor Smith (2nd ed.; New York: Scribner, 1958).—EDITOR.

What Christians Stand For in the Secular World

We cannot command that love. Those who live with God become increasingly filled with it. But none of us can so rely on feeling it as safely to plan his life on the supposition of its emergence when required; and when we consider secular society as a whole we know that we cannot count on it in volume adequate to the need. Indeed in the relationships of politics, commerce, and industry it cannot find expression and can scarcely arise. To this we shall return. What we have to notice at present is that the primary relation between persons—by which in every generation multitudes of men and women have, consciously or unconsciously, guided their lives—has been relegated to a subordinate place by men's headlong eagerness to explore the secrets and exploit the resources of this wonderful universe. In the concentration on wealth we have tended to overlook the more fundamental and more difficult problems of the adjustment of our personal relations to one another.

It is a question whether it was primarily a false understanding of reality that gave free rein to men's egoisms and ambitions; or whether their inherent selfishness inclined them to misread the true nature of things. To whichever cause we assign the greater weight, men's self-centered aims and a false philosophy have cooperated to bring about a profound misunderstanding of the meaning of human life and to create the state of things which we see today.

Science, which has been perhaps the chief influence in giving its distinctive cast and color to the modern consciousness, is essentially an expression of the individualistic approach. As scientist, the individual stands

What Christians Stand For in the Secular World

over against the world, measuring, weighing, experimenting, judging, deciding. The gains which have resulted from this approach and activity are incalculable. We can today only regret this timidity which led Christians in the past to oppose the advances of science. No enlightened Christian today would question the right of science to investigate everything that it is capable of investigating. It is certain that the problems of our complex society cannot be mastered without a continuous expansion of scientific knowledge, more particularly in the field of social sciences.

It is none the less vital for the health of society that we should realize that, while man is meant to have dominion—and we cannot, therefore, be too thankful for the gift of science as an instrument, and are under an obligation to make the fullest use of it—the scientific attitude is only one approach to reality and not the most fundamental and important. As scientist the individual is monarch; he sits in the seat of judgment and asks what questions he will. But the situation is fundamentally changed when he encounters another person who, like himself, is monarch in relation to the world of things. In the encounter with another person or group he is no longer free to ask what questions he will and to order things according to his choice. Questions may be *addressed* to him from a source over which he has no control, and he has to *answer.* He is no longer sole judge, but is subject himself to judgment.

This profound difference between these two approaches to reality, which are uninterchangeable, is often

What Christians Stand For in the Secular World

hidden from us, because it is always possible to bring the relations between persons into the framework of the self-centered view. After the collision has taken place we can reflect upon it and fit it into our picture of the world. At any moment we can step out of the arena of conflict and take our place on the spectator's bench. So ingrained has the habit become that, without being aware of it, we continually have recourse to this form of escape. There is an immense deal that we can learn about persons with the aid of science; but so long as we study them medically, psychologically, sociologically, we never *meet* them. And it is precisely in meeting that real life consists.

It will need a strong and sustained effort to emancipate ourselves from the one-sidedness of the individualistic attitude and to penetrate to the full meaning of the truth that the fundamental reality of life is the interplay, conflict, and continuous adjustment of a multitude of different finite points of view, both of individuals and of groups.

Acknowledgment of this truth would create a wholly different spiritual and intellectual climate from that which has prevailed in recent centuries. Men would still strive, no doubt, to gratify their desires and seek their own aggrandizement; they would not desist from the attempt to domineer over others. But these tendencies would be kept within bounds by a public opinion more aware than at present that in pursuing these courses men are doing violence both to their own nature and to the true nature of things. It would be recognized that men can live at peace with one another only if each individual and each group renounces the claim to have the final and decisive word. Society would have restored to it the sanity which comes from an understanding of human finitude.

A decision for sociality as the basic truth of human existence would create an outlook and temper so different from that which has been dominant in the modern era now drawing to its close as to create a new epoch in human history.

Between the decision for God and the decision for neighbor there is a most intimate connection. In the New Testament these are always interwined. We should in all remembrance of God remember also our neighbor, and in all thought of our neighbor think also of God. Our highest act of worship is not a mystic "flight of the alone to the Alone," but a fellowship meal, a Holy Communion. We come before God as "our Father" to whom all his other children have the same right of access; the truth about God is, among other things, his universal Fatherhood. So, too, the truth about our neighbor is not only what he is to us nor what he is in himself, but above all what he is to God. His relationship to God is the ultimate fact about him, and if we are to think rightly about him or act rightly towards him, we must have the relationship full in view. We must cease to think and feel either in the vertical dimension wherein we are related to God, or in the horizontal dimension wherein we are related to our neighbors, and substitute the triangular relationship, God—self—neighbor, neighbor—God—self.

What Christians Stand For in the Secular World

3. For Man as Rooted in Nature

The most important thing about man is his relation to God and to other men. But his life has also been set in a natural order, which is God's creation. A fundamental duty which man owes to God is reverence for the world as God has made it. Failure to understand and acknowledge this is a principal cause of the present ineffectiveness of the Christian witness in relation to the temporal order. It is one of the chief points at which a fundamental change of outlook is demanded from Christians. Our false outlook is most of all apparent in the exploitation of the physical world. As animals we are part of nature, dependent on it and interdependent with it. We must reverence its economy and cooperate with its processes. If we have dominion over it, that is as predominant partners, not as superior beings who are entitled merely to extract from it what gratifies our desires.

There are two major points at which failure to recognize that man's life is rooted in nature and natural associations leads to mistaken and vain attempts to solve the problem of society. The first grave error characteristic of our time is a too exclusive occupation with politics to the neglect of other equally important spheres of human life and activity. It is assumed that the ills from which society is suffering can be cured, if only we have the will and the right aims. It is forgotten that man is not a being ruled wholly by his reason and conscious aims. His life is inextricably interwined with nature and with the natural associations of family and livelihood, tradition, and culture. When the connection with these sources from which the individual life derives nourishment and strength is broken, the whole life of society becomes enfeebled.

Recognition of the vital importance of centers of human life and activity that underlie and precede the sphere of politics must not be made an excuse for evading the political decisions which have to be made in the near future. It is not a way of escape from political responsibility. Far-reaching decisions in the political sphere may be the only means of creating the conditions in which the nonpolitical spheres can regain vitality and health; but the recovery of health in those spheres is in its turn an indispensable preliminary to political sanity and vigor.

The present plight of our society arises in large part from the breakdown formed of these natural forms of association and of a cultural pattern formed to a great extent under Christian influences. New dogmas and assumptions about the nature of reality have taken the place of the old. New rituals of various kinds are giving shape to men's emotional life. The consequence is that while their aims still remain to a large extent Christian, their souls are molded by alien influences. The real crisis of our time is thus not primarily a moral, but a cultural crisis. Insofar as this is true, the remedy is not to be found in what the church is at present principally doing —insisting on ideals—or in efforts to intensify the will to pursue them. The cure has to be sought in the quite different direction of seeking to re-establish a unity between men's ultimate beliefs and habits and their conscious aims.

What Christians Stand For in the Secular World

Christians must free their minds from illusions and become aware of the impotence of moral advice and instruction when it is divorced from the social structures which by their perpetual suggestion form the soul. It must be remembered that when exhortation and suggestion are at variance, suggestion always wins. Christians must take their part in recreating a sound social and cultural life and thereby in healing the modern divided consciousness, in which head and heart have become divorced and men's conscious purposes are no longer in harmony with the forces which give direction and tone to their emotional life.

But, secondly, if Christians are to have a substantial influence on the temporal order, it is not only necessary that they should have a clearer and deeper understanding of the positive, character-forming function of the nonpolitical forms of human association, but their whole approach to social and political questions needs to be much more realistic than it has commonly been in the past. The Christian social witness must be radically dissociated from the idealism which assumes men to be so free spiritually that aims alone are decisive. There is need of a much clearer recognition of the part played in human behavior by subconscious egoisms, interests, deceptions, and determinisms imposed by man's place in nature and history, by his cultural patterns and by his sinfulness.

It has to be recognized that society is made up of competing centers of power, and that the separate existence of contending vitalities, and not only human sinfulness, make the elimination of power impossible. What has to be aimed at is such a distribution and balance of

What Christians Stand For in the Secular World

power that a measure of justice may be achieved even among those who are actuated in the main by egoistic and sinful impulses. It is a modest aim, but observance of political life leaves no doubt that this must be its primary concern.

If Christians are to act with effect in the temporal order, it is necessary, as was said at the beginning, to distinguish more clearly than is commonly done between the two distinct spheres of society and church, or the different realms of law and Gospel. We also need a clearer and deeper understanding of the difference between justice, human love, and Christian charity. The last transcends both justice and human fellowship while it has contacts with each. Associations cannot love one another; a trade union cannot love an employers' federation, nor can one national state love another. The members of one may love the members of the other so far as opportunities of intercourse allow. That will help in negotiations; but it will not solve the problem of the relations between the two groups. Consequently, the relevance of Christianity in these spheres is quite different from what many Christians suppose it to be. Christian charity manifests itself in the temporal order as a supra-natural discernment of, and adhesion to, *justice* in relation to the equilibrium of power. It is precisely fellowship or human love, with which too often Christian charity is mistakenly equated, that is *not* seriously relevant in that sphere. When the two are identified, it is just those who are most honest and realistic in their thinking and practice that are apt to be repelled from Christianity.

What Christians Stand For in the Secular World

There is scarcely any more urgent task before the church than that this whole complex of problems should be thought out afresh, and it is obviously a task which can be successfully undertaken only in the closest relation with the experience of those who are exposed to the daily pressures of the economic and political struggle. The third decision involves a commitment to a new realm in Christian thought and action; the citizen and the churchman should remain distinct though the same individual should be both.

4. For History

It is a question of vital importance whether history makes any fundamental difference to our understanding of reality. The Greek view was that it does not, and through the great thinkers of antiquity the Hellenic view still exercises a powerful influence over the modern mind.

In the Christian view, on the other hand, it is in history that the ultimate meaning of human existence is both revealed and actualized. If history is to have a meaning, there must be some central point at which that meaning is decisively disclosed. The Jews found the meaning of their history in the call of Abraham, the deliverance from Egypt, and the covenant with God following upon it. For Mohammedans the meaning of history has its center in Mohammed's flight from Mecca. For Marxists the culminating meaning is found in the emergence of the proletariat. The Nazis vainly pinned their hopes to the coming of Hitler. For Christians the decisive meaning of history is given in Christ.

What Christians Stand For in the Secular World

Christianity is thus essentially a continuing action in history determining the course of human development. The Christian understanding of history has much closer affinities with the Marxist view, in which all assertions about the nature of man are inseparably bound up with the dynamics of his historical existence, and with other dynamic views of history, which understand the world in terms of conflict, decision, and fate, and regard history as belonging to the essence of existence, than with the interpretations of Christianity in terms of idealistic thought which were lately prevalent.

A decision for history confronts us with two urgent practical tasks. The first is to disabuse the minds of people of the notion, which is widespread, and infects to a large extent current Christian preaching, that Christianity is in essence a system of morals, so that they have lost all understanding of the truth, so prominent in the New Testament, that to be a Christian is to share in a new movement of life, and to cooperate with new regenerating forces that have entered into history.

The second task is to restore hope to the world through a true understanding of the relation of the kingdom of God to history, as a transcendent reality that is continually seeking, and partially achieving, embodiment in the activities and conflicts of the temporal order. Without this faith men can only seek escape from life in modes of thought which, pushed to their logical conclusion, deprive politics, and even the ethical struggle, of real significance, or succumb to a complete secularization of life in which all principles disintegrate in pure relativity, and opportunism is the only wisdom.

5. For the Gospel and the Church

This understanding brings us face to face with the decision whether or not we acknowledge Christ as the center of history. He is for Christians the source and vindication of those perceptions of the true nature of reality which we have already considered. In the tasks of society Christians can and must cooperate with all those, Christians or non-Christians, who are pursuing aims that are in accord with the divinely intended purpose of man's temporal life. But Christians are constrained to believe that in the power of the Gospel of redemption and in the fellowship of the church lies the chief hope of the restoration of the temporal order to health and sanity.

What none but utopians can hope for the secular world should be matter of actual experience in the church. For the church is the sphere where the redemptive act of God lifts men into the most intimate relation with himself and through that with one another. When this is actually experienced the stream of redemptive power flows out from the church through the lives of its members into the society which they influence. But only a church firm in the faith set forth in outline earlier in this essay can give to its members the inspiration which they need for meeting the gigantic responsibilities of this age. Spiritual resources far beyond anything now in evidence will be needed. It may be that the greatness of the challenge will bring home to Christians how impotent they are in themselves, and so lead to that renewal which will consist in re-discovery of the sufficiency of God and manifestation of his power.

2

THE PROBLEM OF POWER

THE problem of power is obviously of first-rate importance for politics, conspicuously for international politics. But the reason why power is a problem is to be found not in politics but in psychology, ethics, and theology. For politics it is just a fact, to be taken account of along with the other facts. If all men alike as individuals and in their several groupings acted by that faculty of reason which sees all questions in the light of universal principles, there would be no problem of power. Every person and every group would use whatever power they possessed in accordance with some generally agreed plan. But men do not behave like that; nor do nations. If they have power, and see an opportunity to use it to their own advantage, they are disposed to do so, often providing some well-sounding moral arguments in which they more than half believe. When they are using power on behalf of a group to which they belong—a trade union, a commercial firm, or a nation—they dwell on the service they are rendering to their clients, to the exclusion of all attention to the

The Problem of Power

injury inflicted on others, and commit injustice with completely untroubled consciences.

Power, in short, constitutes a strong temptation to selfishness. And so much, perhaps, is obvious. But love of power and its exercise is actually a very common and very insidious form of selfishness. It nearly always disguises itself as a desire to do good, and so manages to claim moral credit for a profoundly immoral frame of mind. In its political forms this love of power is particularly dangerous, because it can appeal to the people who as individuals have very little power to accomplish or to enforce their will. The insignificant citizen of a great nation can compensate for his personal unimportance by his sense of dignity as a participator in the power which his country can exercise in relation to its neighbors. Hitler showed uncanny skill in his exploitation of this fact during his rise to power.

Now because all of these perils are inherent in the fact and use of power, many people would like to eliminate it. They speak with sheer condemnation of "power politics." And of course a political condition in which power alone determines everything is a vile political condition; it is one in which every nation or group is out for all it can get, and selfishness is checked only by lack of power to indulge it. But it is a complete folly to suppose that there can be any politics at all which are not to some extent power politics. So long as men, and by consequence nations, are in some degree selfish, so long will their political relations be determined to a great extent by the power of various kinds—social, economic, military—which the several groups can utilize

What Christians Stand For in the Secular World

in the furtherance of their ends. It is one obvious criticism of the peacemakers of 1919 that they paid insufficient regard to the fact of power. They did not ignore it; but they did not allow enough for it. We must avoid that mistake this time.

Sometimes insistence on the immense importance of power is regarded as cynical and unchristian. The Christian, it is suggested, has his hope set on a state of things where no one will impose his will on anyone else but all will live in harmony for love of justice and of one another. Yes; his hope is set on that. But he knows that his hope can be fulfilled only when all men are converted to love of God through Christ, and more thoroughly converted than he is likely to be able to claim that he himself is as yet. The Christian does not begin by thinking that all men will behave justly of their own accord unless circumstances pervert them; he begins with the conviction that "the heart of man is deceitful above all things and desperately wicked," and that nothing is too bad to be regarded as likely if men see a chance to greater advantage for themselves in pleasure, wealth, or power, but above all in power, by recourse to it. History is full of evidence that men will resort to almost any abomination in the hope of gaining or retaining power. Not all men, of course, or our state would be desperate. And our need now is to determine what course is to be pursued by those who recognize as facts the reality, the necessity, and the insidious character of power.

The only ultimate solution is the conversion of mankind, and to that task the church and the individual Christian as a churchman must devote themselves. But

The Problem of Power

the Christian as citizen has his part to play in the meantime—a meantime which lasts literally and precisely till "kingdom come." Obviously he will not repudiate power; that would be merely to leave it in the hands of those who do not accept his principles. His task is to secure that power is subject to law, and in its ultimate form of physical force is used only for the enforcement and maintenance of law. That is accomplished within a civilized society where law is endowed with force in order that all lawless use of force may be prevented. It is futile to urge that all forms of power shall be actually subject to law; power is too ubiquitous for that. The maxim could not be applied to social power and only in part to economic power. To exercise it in the spirit of justice, which is the inner principle of law, is a moral duty; but failure to perform that duty cannot in practice be scheduled as a crime.

The Christian, then, will stand for subjecting force, and other forms of power when appropriate, to the authority of law; and he will stand for what is really the other side of the same principle, namely, the arming of law with force that it may check the lawless use of force. But then the question arises: What is this law to which all force, and in some degree other forms of power, are to be subject? If it is merely the enactment of the state, it cannot do what is wanted of it. The state may enact what is selfish and unjust. In the international field it would anyhow have to be the enactment of an international authority. At present we have not got one; when the war ends in the victory of the United Nations, it is evident that four of these will in fact possess and exercise an overwhelming power. If they remain united they they can insure the peace of the world. They must not renounce their power. To do that would be to shirk a solemn responsibility entrusted to them by history, in which the Christian sees the operation of divine providence. Yet their power will inevitably constitute a temptation to them to use it selfishly. If the law to which they subject their own power is only what they themselves agree upon, they will tend to become tyrannical; then their rule will not be beneficial and they will probably fail even to keep the peace.

The source of that law to which power must be subject is not any government, national or international. It is the righteousness of God. The ultimate authority of a law is not the state which enacted it but its own justice. Normally we should obey the law even when defective in justice, because normally the whole system of law expresses justice in some degree, and the aim of civilized states is that it shall express justice ever more fully. The state therefore which formulates the law must recognize itself as owing allegiance to justice and formulate accordingly. But this will only occur if the citizens of the state themselves regard justice as rightly supreme over the state, and do not regard the state itself as the origin of justice. But this is essentially the democratic conception of the state, for it makes the state itself subject to the judgment of the citizen's conscience.

The way, then, to the solution of the problem of power is to insist, as public opinion can insist, that the organs of public authority—within the nation the state, among the nations whatever authority is constituted—

shall be able to call upon force sufficient to enforce its regulations, but also and quite equally important, those regulations must be framed in the light of that eternal principle of justice to which each man's conscience in some degree bears witness. Justice must have her sword; but the sword must be in the hand of justice.

For Further Reading

Selected Writings by William Temple on Christian Social Ethics

Essays in Christian Politics and Kindred Subjects. New York: Longmans, Green, 1927.

Christianity in Thought and Practice. New York: Morehouse, 1936.

Citizen and Churchman. London: Eyre and Spottiswoode, 1941.

The Hope of a New World. New York: Macmillan, 1941.

Christianity and Social Order. London: Penguin Books, 1942; reissued by SCM Press, 1950.

The Church Looks Forward. New York: Macmillan, 1944.

Studies of Temple's Life and Thought

PECK, W. G. "William Temple as Social Thinker." in W. R. Matthews *et al., William Temple: An Estimate and an Appreciation.* London: Clarke, 1946.

IREMONGER, F. A. *William Temple, Archbishop of Canterbury: His Life and Letters.* New York: Oxford University Press, 1948; abridgement by D. C. Somervell published as Oxford Paperback. The definitive biography.

CRAIG, ROBERT. *Social Concern in the Thought of William Temple.* London: Gollancz, 1963.

CARMICHAEL, JOHN D., and HAROLD S. GOODWIN. *William Temple's Political Legacy: A Critical Assessment.* London: Mowbray, 1963. Severely critical of Temple, from a conservative social and economic standpoint.

FLETCHER, JOSEPH. *William Temple, Twentieth Century Christian.* New York: Seabury, 1963. A comprehensive study.

Related Works

OLDHAM, J. H., and W. A. VISSER 'T HOOFT. *The Church and Its Function in Society.* Chicago: Willett, Clark, 1937. Prepared for the Oxford Conference on Church, Community, and State in 1937; still valuable.

Malvern 1941: The Life of the Church and the Order of Society. London: Longmans, Green, 1942. Proceedings of an important British conference chaired by Temple.

For Further Reading

RECKITT, MAURICE B. (ed.), *Prospect for Christendom: Essays in Catholic Social Reconstruction.* London: Faber, 1945. Product of the "Christendom group," Anglo-Catholic thinkers with whom Temple had many affinities.

RECKITT, MAURICE B. *Maurice to Temple: A Century of the Social Movement in the Church of England.* London: Faber, 1947.

Facet Books Already Published

Social Ethics Series:
1. *Our Calling*
   by Einar Billing (translated by Conrad Bergendoff). 1965
2. *The World Situation*
   by Paul Tillich. 1965
3. *Politics as a Vocation*
   by Max Weber (translated by H. H. Gerth and C. Wright Mills). 1965
4. *Christianity in a Divided Europe*
   by Hanns Lilje. 1965
5. *The Bible and Social Ethics*
   by Hendrik Kraemer. 1965
6. *Christ and the New Humanity*
   by C. H. Dodd. 1965
7. *What Christians Stand For in the Secular World*
   by William Temple. 1965
8. *Legal Responsibility and Moral Responsibility*
   by Walter Moberly. 1965

Biblical Series:

1. *The Significance of the Bible for the Church*
   by Anders Nygren (translated by Carl Rasmussen). 1963
2. *The Sermon on the Mount*
   by Joachim Jeremias (translated by Norman Perrin). 1963
3. *The Old Testament in the New*
   by C. H. Dodd. 1963
4. *The Literary Impact of the Authorized Version*
   by C. S. Lewis. 1963
5. *The Meaning of Hope*
   by C. F. D. Moule. 1963
6. *Biblical Problems and Biblical Preaching*
   by C. K. Barrett. 1964
7. *The Genesis Accounts of Creation*
   by Claus Westermann (translated by Norman E. Wagner). 1964

8. *The Lord's Prayer*
   by Joachim Jeremias (translated by John Reumann). 1964
9. *Only to the House of Israel? Jesus and the Non-Jews*
   by T. W. Manson. 1964
10. *Jesus and the Wilderness Community at Qumran*
    by Ethelbert Stauffer (translated by Hans Spalteholz). 1964
11. *Corporate Personality in Ancient Israel*
    by H. Wheeler Robinson. 1964
12. *The Sacrifice of Christ*
    by C. F. D. Moule. 1964
13. *The Problem of the Historical Jesus*
    by Joachim Jeremias (translated by Norman Perrin). 1964

Body, 12 on 14 Garamond
Display, Garamond
Paper: White Spring Grove E.F.